To TAVISTOCK GOOSIE FAIR

CLIVE GUNNELL

'For the people of Tavistock with thanks.'

BOSSINEY BOOKS

First published in 1978
by Bossiney Books
St Teath, Bodmin, Cornwall
Typeset and printed in Great Britain by
Penwell Ltd, Parkwood, Callington,
Cornwall

ISBN 0 906456 06 1

Plate Acknowledgements

Cover photograph — T. Freeman

Westward Television 20
Rob Fogwell 14, 16, 17
Stanley M. Green 4, 26, 27
Thorington Photographs 1-3, 8, 9, 15, 18, 19, 21-25, 28-30, 38-41
Gordon Moore (courtesy of Westward Television) 7
Roger Edwards 6

Old Photos of the Fair were kindly lent by Maurice Jones, David Thomas and Mrs. E. Treglown and the music of the Goosie Fair Song by Tom Brown.

ABOUT THE AUTHOR

Clive Gunnell *lives in his three-hundred-year-old cottage, just outside Tavistock. In this, his second book, he takes us to Tavistock Goosie Fair* and *on a very personal conducted tour of the ancient Stannary Town. Writing with insight and affection, he brings to life one of the country's most historic Fairs and introduces us to some of the characters who make it such an event in the Westcountry calendar.*

Few men are better qualified to write on the subject. Apart from living there nearly twenty years, in 1977 he won the Pye TV International Award for the best regional documentary with his Westward film on the Fair, the presentation being made by Sir Harold Wilson at the Dorchester. Since joining Westward, Clive Gunnell has produced, written, directed and presented a whole string of memorable documentaries.

In 1975 he collaborated with Sir John Betjeman, Charles Causley, J.C. Trewin and others to write Both Sides of Tamar, *Bossiney Books' portrait of Devon and Cornwall in words and pictures. Then in 1977 his book* My Dartmoor *was immediately hailed as one of the finest volumes ever written about the Moor.*

FOREWORD

It gives me great pleasure to write the Foreword of this book, *To Tavistock Goosie Fair* by Clive Gunnell. Firstly, because I am proud to have such a distinguished and interesting writer and TV personality as Clive Gunnell living in my Constituency. Secondly, because Tavistock Goosie Fair is one of the highlights of the year for our part of the world. Clive Gunnell has captured the fun and enjoyment of this great day in Tavistock in his book. It would be a sad day if traditions and 'fun days' like this disappeared from our scene in this modern age. I hope it will continue for a long time to come and those who cannot get to the fair, read this book and you will catch something of what Goosie Fair means to us Devonians. Well done and many thanks Clive Gunnell, now you are one of us!

PETER MILLS
September 1978

To TAVISTOCK GOOSIE FAIR

'It seem'd to we all Dev'n must be to Tavvystock Goozey Vair,' sang Ned 'Annafurd, Jan Steer and Nicky Square over fifty years ago. Were they with us today, their words would have even more meaning, for the crowds get larger and larger. People come not merely from Devon, but from all over the country and they come just so they can return home and say, 'We've been to Tavistock Goosie Fair.'

Why?

Because it's great fun, it's a fair for people, about people, involving people of all ages enjoying themselves in a manner they have done for centuries, a manner that totally excludes the crudeness, vulgarity and expense so essential in modern fields of entertainment. It's a time when country comes to town, not only produce and livestock, but country people, moorland farmers, their wives and children, families up from Cornwall visiting relatives, all renewing and re-affirming old friendships. For most of the farming community, Goose Fair means a harvest safely gathered in and a brief moment of relaxation before the rigours of winter farming commence in earnest.

For the children of the area, however, Goose Fair begins with the arrival in Bedford Square on Tuesday evening of the 'Golden Gallopers', a unique nineteenth century roundabout, resplendent in the primitive decoration of the showman's art, with brightly painted carved horses and a shining polished Gavioli organ. This has by recent tradition become the first of the entertainments in operation at dawn light on Goose Fair morning and is besieged by youngsters clamouring for rides.

From that moment Tavistock concentrates on enjoying itself. The school children, given a day's holiday, pack the Square bringing their parents with them on the understanding they behave themselves. All are filled with the same joyous sense of urgency and excitement.

This normally peaceful Stannary town has overnight transformed itself into a hive of entertainment: generators throb; candy striped awnings cover fun fairs and stalls; there are roundabouts for all ages, hot dogs and candy floss, bingo and hoop-la, helter skelter and children's slides. Market traders with blankets, china, toys and games, sell their wares, they say, at bargain prices never again to be equalled. And riding high above the crowd, enormous gas-filled balloons, all colours of the rainbow, strain at their strings to escape and ride the heather-scented updraughts of Dartmoor's valleys and tors.

Everywhere there are people, jostling and shouting, pushing and shrieking; sisters, cousins, aunts and nieces, who have not seen each other this past twelvemonth, embrace amidst screams of delight and recognition; farmers greet in warm affection those they have haggled and argued with all year over cattle deals in Devon's markets; and louder and more commanding than all the rest, the foreign tongues of itinerant 'cheap jacks' fill the air with unstoppable sales patter.

' 'Ere, this box of perfume, good gear, straight up, no messing . . . in Boots, the Chemist, this morning they were knocking em a'at for ten nicker . . . straight up missus, I'm not kidding. What do you think I'm asking for it? Go on, 'ave a guess? Not ten pa'and, that's certain, not five pa'and, not even free pa'and . . . 'ere, this lot, one quid, one pa'and note. Ain't no-one prepared to take a chance? Lady at the back, you 'ave one luv, good luck to yer lady, best buy you'll have this week, no messing. 'Ere, annuver lady over there, annuver . . . always said Devon people knew a bargain when they saw one. What's that luv, you come from Clapham, aw my Gawd!'

Tavistock Goose Fair, however, is something more than just a day of pleasure. It's a time for stocktaking, of assessing business success or failure during the past year, for discussing the innovations and improvements implemented by farming friends and rivals, for hearing the much-embroidered stories of farming profit and loss. But most of all for unlimited gossip. For many it is also the day they settle outstanding debts to traders in the town. 'Right me 'andsome, we'll settle with 'ee. How much does us owe 'ee, doan't forget the discount for cash.'

'They always add that extra bit of Devon logic,' said Ernest Knape, ex Town Councillor and a Tavistock Chemist for over forty years, 'but they always come in first thing and pay cash. They don't want anything to interfere with their day out, particularly their goose dinners. These were always a most important part of the fair in the old days. Not only did every pub and hotel put on goose dinners, but outsiders would rent empty shops and serve dinners. Of course, not everyone could afford goose, so the less scrupulous would buy rabbits which were always plentiful and cheap, bleach them, cook them in goose fat and sell them as genuine goose dinners.'

In Duke Street the aroma of freshly ground coffee entices the visitor into Norman Creber's delicatessen. 'In my father's day, Goose Fair always meant extra work, for we would fill the shop window with 'fairings', especially large pink and white sugared almonds. They were a tradition for years. We would sell hundreds of pounds of fairings, a pound for mum, a pound for gran, a pound for each of the children. Stalls in the market square would also sell fairings. Then there would be small sticks of cinnamon covered in sugar, and ginger nuts, another fair day speciality, but for some reason this tradition seems to have disappeared since the war.'

For many years Mary Warne kept the Royal Standard at Mary Tavy with husband Bill and on fair day she would sing every verse of *Tavistock Goozey Vair* in notes clear as a bell.

'Well, you see, as a girl I lived in the Peter Tavy Inn — my father kept it — and I learnt every word of the Goose Fair song from the old men who sang it round the fire. I wasn't born there. I was born in the Old Toll House at Grenofen, historical old place 'twas. It was pulled down and vanished overnight to make more room for motorcars — crying shame that was. I remember on Goose Fair morning, when us children left the house to walk into Tavistock, us could hear the fairground music coming up from the wharf as we went down the hill, and we would get excited and our feet quickened in anticipation. That was our first indication of fair day. Oh, I remember, when us got there, a wonderful man who came from Plymouth who could eat fire — we would watch spellbound as the fire came out of his mouth — and a sword swallower who could lose long sharp swords right down inside his stomach. There was a man called Strong who sold his own medicine that could cure anything; no matter what you had wrong, his medicine could cure it.'

Creber's delicatessen is situated immediately opposite what used to be the most popular pub in Tavistock, The White Hart, where I've enjoyed many a good pint. Today it's an estate agents, a unique example of modern vandalism. From his bedroom window above the shop, Norman Creber, as a young boy, could watch the world go by on Goose Fair day in perfect safety, peeping through a hole in the wooden shutters into the windows of the White Hart.

'It was always full of sailors. They would come up on the train from Plymouth, and you've never seen such drinking and carrying on. Of course, there would always be fights with the local lads. On Goose Fair morning the first thing they did was take the pub doors off, unscrew the hinges and take the doors away — that way they could always get them out. Many of them would be flung out, right through the doorway into the gutter without bouncing. They had their own chuckers out and they must have been very good for I never saw one bounce.'

Bill Warne also recalls The White Hart. 'Thirty five years ago I came in on my motorbike Goose Fair day and put it round the back of The White Hart and knocked on the door. The landlord, Stanley Goode, opened it and he looked dreadful. I asked him what was the matter. 'Come on in here,' he said, 'and see what they've done.' There were piles of glasses higher than my head and he hadn't got a light in the place. He had candles on the bar as they'd knocked all the lights off. They'd ripped down everything from the walls, mirrors, pictures, everything — you've never seen such a shambles. Of course, they used to be open all day then and that's when they decided to stop it and close during the afternoon. That made it better for everybody, particularly the publicans, as it gave them a break and believe me, they needed it.'

One of the real pleasures of Goose Fair for the residents of Tavistock came when the day had almost drawn to its close. Then those in the know would rush up the hill to Tavistock North railway station to watch the visitors from Plymouth, Brentor, Lydford, Bridestowe and Okehampton catch their trains. 'It was a scream,' remembers Ernest Knape. 'Some of them were so drunk they didn't know where they lived or which train to get on. Some would be seen off by Tavistock friends who were in a worse state than they were, and who generally ended up aboard the train with them. The station platform was always knee deep in litter. You had to wade through it to make any progress and often you would stumble over someone who had decided to go to sleep on the platform. These people would be carried on to the train generally to wake up at Exeter and realise they had only gone to the station to see off a friend. Then they would

1. Nicola Gunnell on Fair Day

2. The Author with his Pye International TV Award

3. Filming the Fair

4. Auctioneer Tom Brown rings the bell

5. On the Day

6 & 7 With Donald Phillips, the Farmers' Friend

8. Farmer John Doidge

9. Nicola Gunnell coming down

▲ 10. 1903

11. 1912 ▼

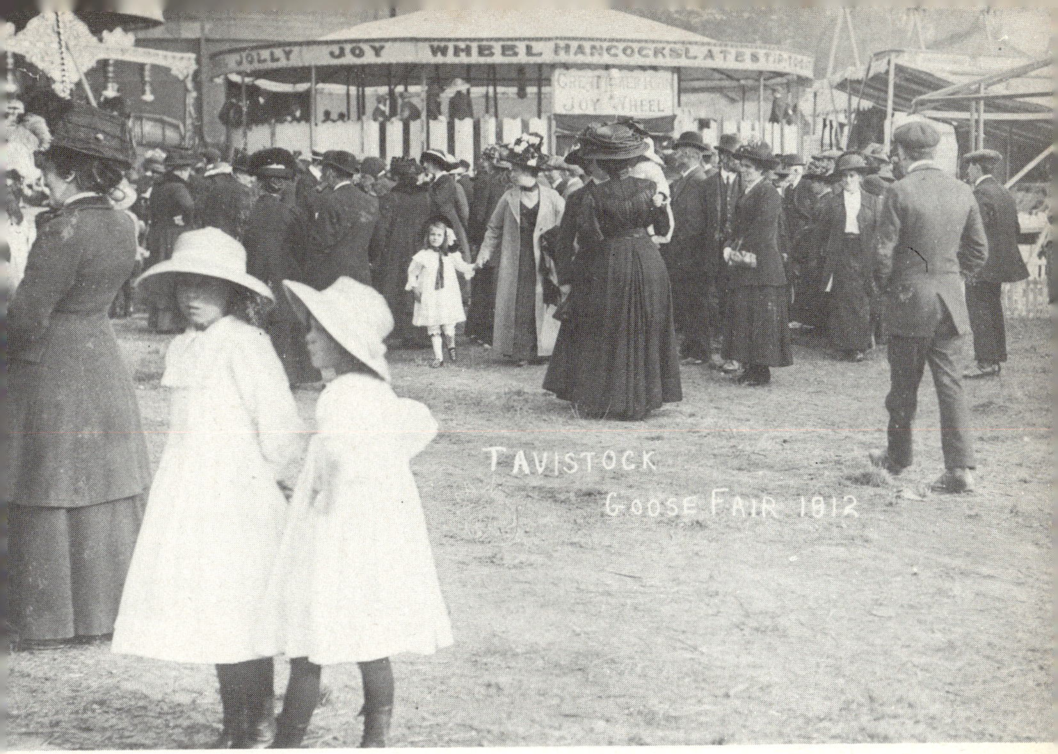
JOLLY JOY WHEEL HANCOCKS LATEST
JOY WHEEL
TAVISTOCK
GOOSE FAIR 1812

12. & 13. 1912

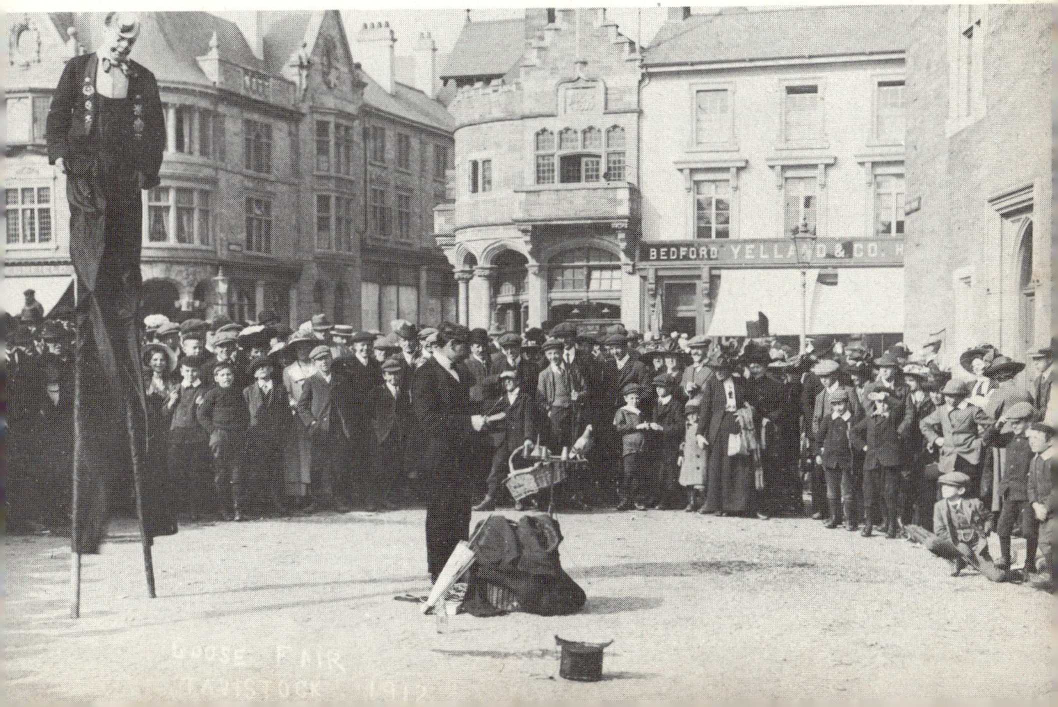
BEDFORD YELLAND & CO.
GOOSE FAIR
TAVISTOCK 1912

14. & 15. All the Fun of the Fair

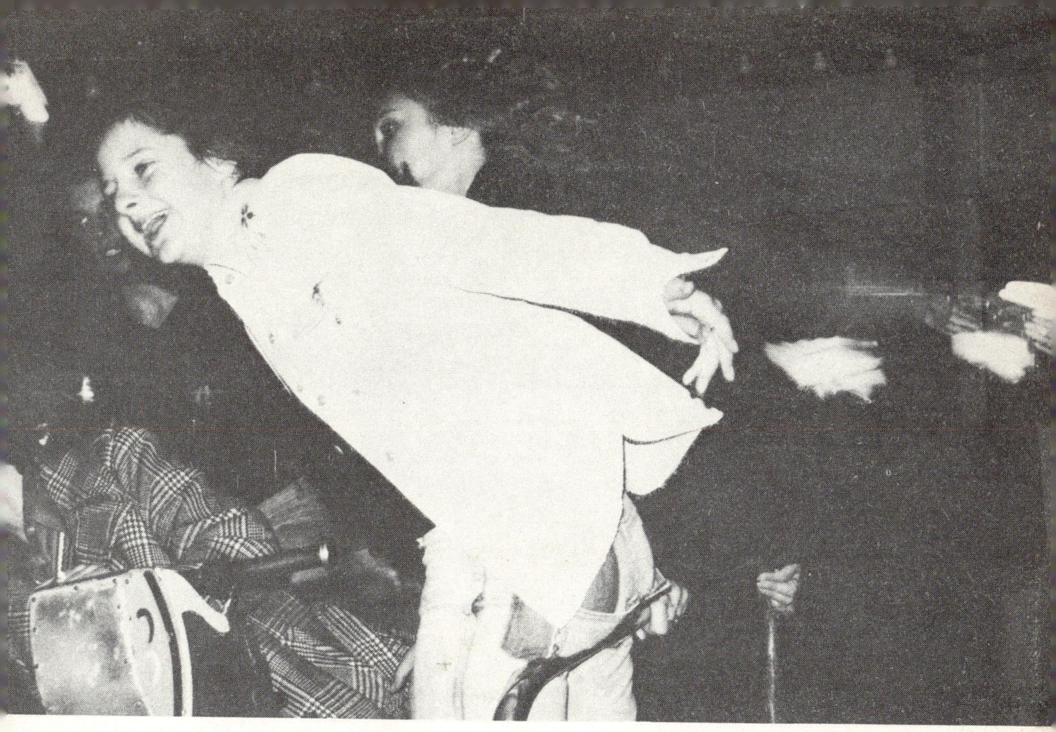

16. & 17. Expressions

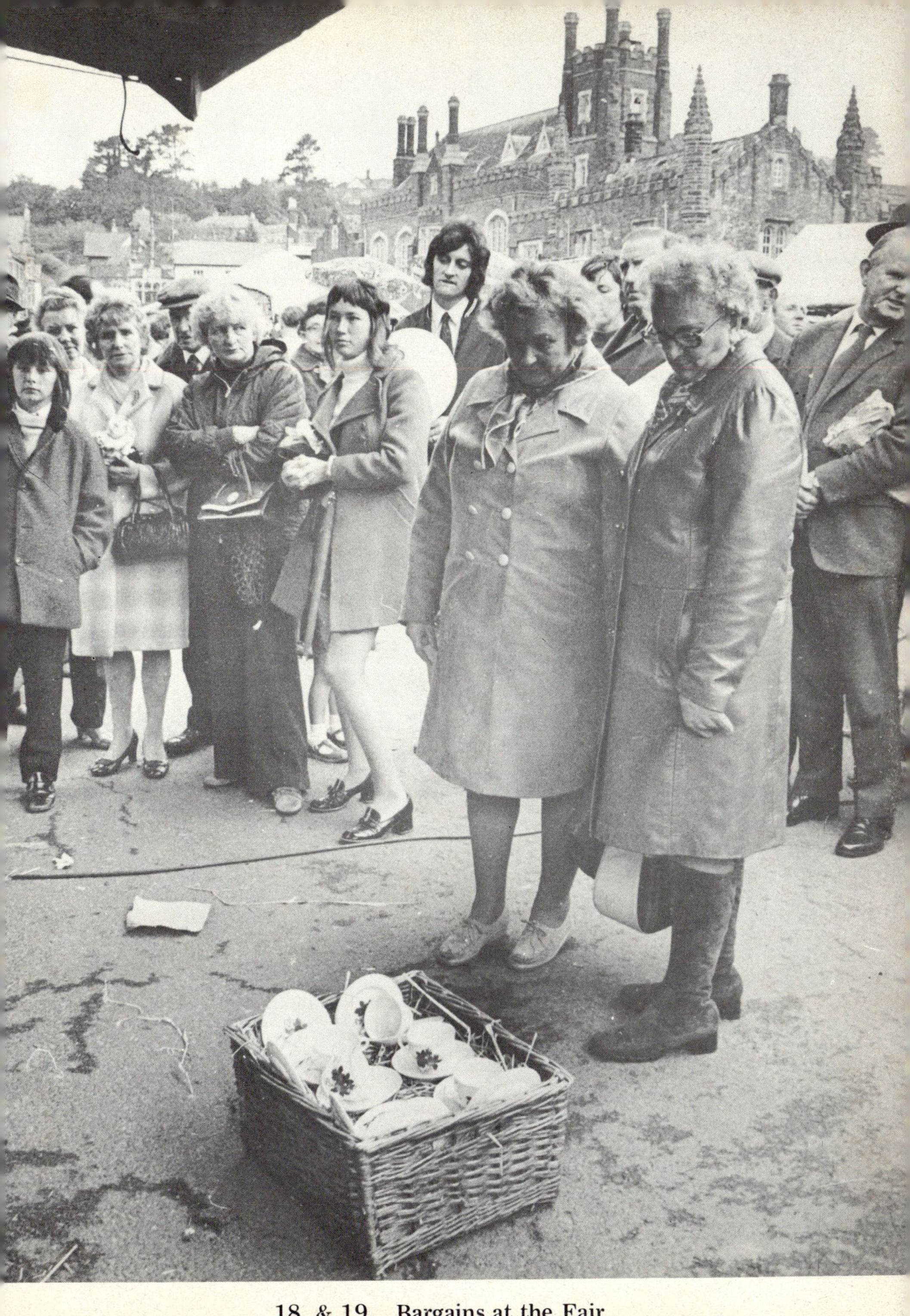

18. & 19. **Bargains at the Fair**

20. One of the few geese at the Fair today

have to try and make their way back home to Tavistock. Some people would even run from Tavistock North to Tavistock South and watch it all happening over again.'

The real reason for Goose Fair, however, has nothing to do with any of these happenings, and to watch it taking place you must elbow your way through the dense crowd crammed together between the stalls and stands that today stretch along the Whitchurch Road almost to the cattle market, where the serious business of buying and selling cattle and sheep, ponies and poultry is in progress.

All day enormous cattle wagons roar backwards and forwards through the town up to the cattle market to disgorge cattle down their ramps. Drovers with unintelligible cries direct them with sharp pokes and occasional whacks into metal barred pens which they leave only for show and sale.

'Now come on gentlemen, come on, you can do better than that. This fine animal can't be sold for that price. Now gentlemen, do I hear 185 . . . 185 gentlemen, yes, 188, 190, 195, do I hear 200, gentlemen 200, no, going then for 195 once, 195 twice, sold for 195 Prentice.' And the wise old farmers leaning over the bars of the auction ring nod knowingly across the pen to each other.

Suddenly there is uproar behind us, shouts and curses, and an animal, more intelligent than the rest or reluctant to acknowledge the herd instinct, makes a break for freedom. Sticks are banged on metal bars, creating panic and confusion, until the poor creature, twisting and turning in bewilderment, is finally cornered and driven back up the ramp into the wagon.

'The cattle used to come to market on foot along with the other livestock,' recalls farmer John Doidge, leaning over the sale ring eagerly watching the sale of his bullocks. He is now in his eighty-third year, a fresh cut rose in his button hole. 'We used to have to gather 'n in by lantern light and drive 'n in using lanterns. In they days us wouldn't put the ponies up for sale in the market. They were all sold private. A man's word was good enough and a drink would settle the business. Course, the market would open six in the morning and the ponies would be in little bunches from Abbey Garage right out to Whitchurch Down — each one had their herd of ponies. Of course, driving 'n in you'd miss 'n, say a sheep or two, and you'd have to go back and look for they afterwards. It used to be 'andsome to see all they cottagers who used to keep a few geese driving 'n in along the road. Pretty near all the people kept geese then, now they'm very scarce. A lot of Cornish buyers used to come to see me Goose Fair and always buy me a drink. Well, you see, I used to do a lot of business buying calves for they Cornish around Princetown fair time. You see now Princetown's gone, Callington's gone — 'tis a shame for those things to die out I think — it brings the people together and they know your town's on the map, don't they?'

'Funniest thing I ever saw Goose Fair,' remembers Bill Warne, 'was a man from Bere Alston — I won't tell 'ee 'is name, he's still alive. He brought his horse in here to market and he sold it, and then walked around for a time before deciding to look for another horse to buy. He saw this horse in the middle of the market yard, all clipped, looking very well and asked, "What do you want for the horse?" They told 'n, he bought it, saddled 'n up and rode it down to the White Hart, stayed a while, had a few beers, and then rode home. When he got home, he jumped off the horse and shouted to his wife, "Come and tell me what you think of my new horse", and the horse walked across the farmyard and straight into the stable. He'd bought his own horse — he couldn't recognise it. The gypsies had worked on it and had then sold it back to him for two guineas more than they gave for it!'

AUCTIONEER TOM BROWN

The most important job in the cattle market throughout fair day is that of auctioneer and for the past fifty years this has been the responsibility of Tom Brown, a man known, respected, and loved by all who have come into contact with him. He is still doing occasional work with the firm of Ward and Chowen which he joined in the 30s.

'They say farmers are difficult people to get along with, but I can honestly say that in fifty years I've never had any trouble, the odd argument now and then, of course, but never what you might call real trouble. You see, Goose Fair always was, and for that matter still is, predominantly a farming fair, the other things have grown out of it. Dartmoor acts as a reservoir for livestock. They come off the moor after grazing all summer for the autumn sales and Goose Fair was only one of those sales. Princetown Fair, you see, that was a good sale. We would sell all the local farm livestock first and then in the afternoon at 2 p.m. we would sell off the Prison cattle, all their stock, good stock it was too, even the wool would be auctioned that day.

'Of course, when I began all the stock was driven into market. The whole area around on Tuesday night would be lit for miles by hurricane lamps and the swearing of drovers and the barking of dogs. They would drive them right up to the market gate. For years the first person to arrive would be Dinah Tuckett from Dunnabridge Pound, the other side of Two Bridges. It was very important, you see, to be among the first to arrive. The idea, of course, was to get what were considered the best pens in the market — the middle pens were ideal for it was in the middle part of the day when trade really started livening up. Around four in the morning they would start arriving and to do this, of course, Dinah would have had to leave the farm and start driving in around midnight.

'There were always plenty of geese then. Dressed geese would be brought to the pannier market on Tuesday before Goose Fair and sold to hotels and private individuals who held Goose Fair parties. Live geese were sold in the cattle market. They came in from outlying farms and cottages on the moor where most of them held goose and gander rights similar to the grazing rights for cattle, ponies and sheep of Commoners today which entitled them to run geese on the moor for grazing. The geese came to market in carts, sometimes as many as sixty carts would be lined up all with the heads and long necks of the geese sticking out through the wires — a pretty sight it looked — they would sell for six to seven shillings a piece then. It was the fowl pest law put an end to geese coming to market. We hardly see any now — it's a great pity.

'Everybody had a goose dinner in they days. We used to have a famers' lunch before the war. There used to be a man called Sammy Stone had a temperance hotel in King Street and we held it there to start with, and then he moved to the Union and so we held them there. Two hundred farmers we would entertain — free goose dinners. One partner would come down with them for an hour at 11.30 and then go back to market and let the other partner join them. We would reckon one goose for six farmers.

'Goose Fair was big business. All the buyers would attend from everywhere, for it was always well advertised. We had accommodation for 2,000 head of stock in the pens, but you see sometimes we would have 3,500 or 4,000 head. We would have to get pens from Dousland and they would stretch right up Down Road on the grass verge to Whitchurch Down, and we would hold an overflow market in Pixon Lane.

'I've enjoyed it all, every second of it, and friends, I've made so many friends. Not a great deal has changed on the moor, you see, the old names are still there and in my working life I've dealt with four generations of some Dartmoor farming families and hope to go on long enough to do business with a fifth.

'I remember one old farmer used to farm out to Okehampton, never missed a Goose Fair. Year after year he would meet old friends, have a drink with each one, and return home without a care in the world. On the way he would stop at the Dartmoor Inn, Lydford. You see, the only way his wife would let him come to Goose Fair was to do business, so he would say he was going to sell the old ram. He would take it as far as the Dartmoor Inn, leave it in the field at the back and pick it up again on his way home, telling his wife he couldn't get a fair price for 'n. He got away with this story for years.'

FARMER JOHN

John Doidge, known to everyone in Tavistock as Farmer John, can recall almost eighty years of Goose Fair but his earliest memory is a sad one.

'I came to my first Goose Fair at six years old. My fairther gave me a new sixpence and when I arrived to Goosie Fair and came to spend 'n, I discovered a hole in me pocket and the sixpence gone. I searched for fairther all day but never did find 'n. I a'ant never forgot that first Goosie Fair day and how miserable I was.

'The funniest thing that happened to me fair day — I bought a calf and I was bringing 'n home, in a hurry because I wanted to take my wife back to the fair, and when I got home I hanged back a bit and the halter rope went slack and slipped over its neck and he turned around and ran all the way back to the cattle market. He knew where his mother was that he'd 'ave left and I had to run all back to Tavvy and catch 'un. We had to lead 'n all in they days y'see. There was a lot of horse trading, 'cause all the gypsies would be here. They would camp on the moor and 'twas their annual get together for the year, to buy and sell horses and ponies, drink in all the pubs and afterwards they would fight, terrible fights they had. The biggest policemen in Devon would be on duty that day I can tell 'ee.

''Twas they gypsies stole me as a babe. Fairther had summons'd 'em for stealing his sheep and to pay him back they stole me out of my cot. I was only eighteen months old, and they took me with'm when they left Tavistock. Course, being real gypsies they couldn't hurt a babe, so when they arrived to Postbridge on the moor, they left me in the middle of the road. Y'see they knew Norman Gregory would be along directly driving the Unicorn (the dray) — 'twas all 'oss driven in they days — delivering the beer. 'Twere raining hard when he found me, but he knew I had been kept dry for not even my little booties were damp. They say when the Police told mother I'd been found, she leapt into the trap without touching the step. I was the first born, d'you see. She must have thought she may not get another. Of course, I don't believe it had anything to do with fairther they stole me, I say 'twas to improve their breed.'

THE FARMERS' FRIEND

Louder and with greater urgency than the cry of the auctioneer, drovers and wagon drivers, another voice can be plainly distinguished above all other noises of the market. 'Now, I bought these boots direct from the British Government, eight hundred pairs, and there isn't a bad pair among 'em, real leather soles and genuine calfskin uppers, you couldn't buy better boots than these anywhere in the land, worth over twelve pounds at today's prices. D'you know what I'm asking? Well, I'm not even asking £5, not £1.75 not even £1.60, I'm selling these boots for £1.50, go on look at 'em, hold 'em in your hands if you like. Fellow over there wants two pairs, one for Sunday, one for weekdays. Donald Phillips, that's me, known to everyone as the "Farmers' Friend". Every fair, market and county show in the South West knows me. I come from Exeter and so did my father, that's my father's name up there on the wagon — George. He was born before me. He was a wealthy man my father, owned thirty two houses in Exeter and he made all his money out of farmers.

'My father used to come to Goosie Fair until he was ninety years old. He began by driving the horses and wagon over the moorland roads in the dark passing hundreds of geese being driven in flocks by their owners, each gaggle illuminated by its own flickering hurricane lamp. I've been coming here over forty years and in all that time I've done all my business with farmers. You know farmers are always grumbling that times are bad and they have no money, but I'll tell you something about farmers; their cheques are beautiful. I've never had a bad cheque from a farmer, not one.

'Now, d'you see this raincoat, I've only got one of these left. I've had over five hundred, made for Royal Marine Officers they were, now there's only one thing wrong with this coat. It's got a button off. You can have this coat for six pounds. Now who wants it — what nobody. Damn the devil, I wish he were dead. You want this coat, sir? Yes . . . I said yes once and it cost me a damn sight more than six pounds. D'you know last year at the Devon County Show a farmer came up to me and said he had a complaint to make. He said he bought a coat from me and the top button had come off. I asked him when he bought it and he said twenty years ago. Damn me if all that happens to a coat is a button comes off after twenty years, there can't be much I sell here to complain about, can there? I'm going to leave you all now, yes, I'm going to have my Goose lunch. That's all I come to Goosie Fair for, my meal of Goose. Wouldn't miss that not for all the money in the world.'

Donald Phillips, leaving his wares in the capable hands of his brothers, forces his way through the dense crowds back towards Tavistock, where the crowded pubs, overflowing on to the pavements outside, are having their busiest day of the year. In the Cornish Arms a coach trip from Plymouth complete with comic hats have taken over the public bar and are holding a concert with piano and microphone. *Nellie Dean* has received her sixth rendition of the day and couples, who a few hours earlier were complete strangers, are now, with arms locking waists, doing a 'knees-up' around the tables. In the saloon bar, customers struggle over, round and through each other to obtain service and then, balancing drinks, goose rolls and sandwiches precariously on metal trays, wriggle back to their seats.

The hosts, Margaret and Bert Wood, hot and tired, diplomatic but firm, friendly yet keeping an eye cocked for the slightest hint of trouble, gaze perpetually at the clock and the hands ticking remorselessly towards closing time and the chance to get their feet up and rest before the evening's performance renews the day's activities and the onslaught begins again.

By evening a long train of motorcars from Plymouth, trying to enter Tavistock for the fair, winds back from Drake's statue, past the Harvest Home at Grenofen. A harrassed overworked, understaffed Police force somehow manage to keep through traffic moving and disperse the remainder to carparks and possible parking positions anywhere about the town. The pubs, already packed and bulging at the seams, somehow expand to admit even more. The streets are jammed with crowds walking shoulder to shoulder, ten abreast from pavement to pavement, and everywhere there is noise and excitement, all illuminated by fairy lights and flood lamps. The screams of women on the Ben Hur and dodgems mingle with the exhortations of street traders and cheap jacks, the non-stop urgings of sideshow and stall owners to 'try your luck, luv', and the shouts of over-excited children will continue until past midnight, when the last visitors slowly and reluctantly make their way home. Only then do the stallholders and traders begin breaking down stands and packing away goods and when the first glimmer of dawn lights the tors of Dartmoor, all that remains is a mountain of rubble and refuse knee deep around the town. Even this will have disappeared by the time the first businessmen and bank managers arrive for another busy day at the office. The town can relax until Goose Fair returns again next year.

NOTTINGHAM GOOSE FAIR

By a strange coincidence although I have been involved with Tavistock Goose Fair for a number of years it was not the first such fair I attended — that was Nottingham Goose Fair.

I came to Nottingham Playhouse after the war as Master Carpenter from Manchester Repertory Company. It was not the costly palatial example of contemporary architecture that graces the city today. It was a small theatre, converted from a cinema with no packing or flying space, but productions from this building under the direction of André Van Gyseghem, introduced names who are today internationally known but were then on the threshold of their careers: Maxine Audley, Leo McKern, Michael Aldridge, Alfred Burke and many more. They laid the foundation for everything that followed.

These were good days, demobbed from the war, no responsibility, enjoyable, creative employment with a stage set to build every two weeks; a beautiful city with even more beautiful girls. There was plenty of entertainment too; Tommy Lawton and Frank Broome playing together, and I mean together, for Notts County — who were Nottingham Forest? — Ken Mackintosh and his band voted Melody Maker big band of the year and Chick Zamick playing ice hockey.

Then came Nottingham Goose Fair, the first since it had been stopped by the war. I had never seen anything quite like it before. It seemed to stretch for miles across the enormous park and recreation ground known as the Forest, and, of course, there were the machines, roundabouts and side-shows which we had all forgotten. It provided absolute proof that the war was really over: a golden experience that I will always remember with great joy.

There are many similarities in the history of the two fairs. The celebration of the Feast of St Matthew is generally accepted as the origin of Nottingham Goose Fair, a festivity well established in 1284 when the Charter of King Edward I first referred to Nottingham's fairs. In 1541 Goose Fair was first mentioned in the Borough records when the Chamberlain's accounts included an item: an allowance of 1s 10d for twenty two stalls the Sheriffs had on Goose Fair Day.

The Fair was held on the Feast of St Matthew, the Apostle, September 21st, until 1752 when the revision of the calendar meant losing eleven days from the month of September and Goose Fair Day was changed to October 2nd. Then the Fair lasted eight days but in 1876 it was reduced to five days and four years after this date it was reduced again — to three days.

Today Nottingham Goose Fair is held on the first Thursday, Friday and Saturday in October on a site specially allocated on the Forest Recreation Ground where the Fair covers eighteen acres. Like Tavistock Fair, the prime function of Nottingham Goose Fair was originally that of trade, and it was for many years a Cheese Fair, but its legendary origins are still those of gaggles of geese driven to Nottingham along the roads from Norfolk and Lincolnshire to be sold at the market. Still today on the first day of the fair, sales of breeding sheep and rams are held in the Cattle Market, along with sales of pedigree pigs.

Nottingham Goose Fair is officially opened at noon on the Thursday by the Chief Executive and Town Clerk reading a Proclamation in the presence of the Sheriff of Nottingham, after which the Lord Mayor rings a pair of silver bells and the festivities commence.

Perhaps one day the elegant Midlands city and the Devon country town might exchange civic dignitaries for the opening of their respective Fairs and establish a bond of friendship to match the history they share through holding the best fairs in England.

21. Fishing on the Tavy

22. Jubilee Arch

23. Tavistock on a non-Fair day

24. The same ground on Fair Day

25. Salesmanship

26 & 27 Old Market scenes

28. The Still Tower

29. The Abbey ruins

"Tavvystock Goozey Vair"

Words and Music:

C. John Trythall

No. 1 in F

No. 2 in G.

PRICE 2/- NET

J. H. LARWAY,
Proprietors : EDWIN ASHDOWN, LTD.,
19, HANOVER SQUARE, LONDON, W.1
MADE AND PRINTED IN ENGLAND.

TAVVYSTOCK GOOZEY VAIR.

Words and Music by C. JOHN TRYTHALL.

made our-sels quite 'vit-ty' Us shav'd and grais'd our 'air An'
off us goes in our Zun-day cloes be-'ind Bill's ole gray mare. Us
smell'd the sage an' on-ions arl th' way fr'm Whit-church Down, An'
didn' us av a blaw-out when us put up in th' town, An'

mf
theer us met Ned 'An-na-furd, Jan_ Steer an' Nick-y Square,_ Ut
mf
cresc.
sim to we arl Deb'm mus' be to Tav-vy-stock Goo-zey Vair._ An' uts
cresc.
f
Aw thun, whur be'e gwaine,_ an' wot be'e do-in' of there?_ 'Aive
f
ff
down yer prong, an' stap down long, tes Tav-vy-stock Goo-zey Vair._
rall.
ff
rall.
mf

p
Us
Twus
went an' zeed th' 'oss - es, an' th' yaf - fers, an' th' yaws, Us
rain - in' straims an' dark as pitch when us start - ed 'ome that night An'
went 'pun arl th' round - a - bouts an' in - ter arl th' shaws An'
when us got pas' Mer - ri - val Birdge' th' mare er tuk a vright Says
then ut start - ed rain - in' 'an blaw - in' too, Es Fai, So
I to Bill, "Be care - ful er you'll av us in th' drains" Says

off us goes back to th' 'Rose' an' 'aves a dish o' tay An'
Bill ter me, "Be - gad," says 'e, "Why, abm' yew got th' reins?" Just
then us 'ad a zing - zong an' th' folks kep' drap-pin' in. An'
then th' mare run slap a - gin a whack-in' gurt big stoan 'Er
them wot knaw'd us arl cum roun' an' 'ad a drap o' gin Till
kicked th' trap to flib - bits an 'er trot - ted off a - lone When
wot with one an' toth - er us did - n' sim to care
us cum to us reck - in'd twarnt no gude set - tin' there So us
mf

LOWE & BRYDONE PRINTERS LTD., LONDON, N.W. 10

GOOSE FAIR AND THE ABBEY OF TAVISTOCK

The towns of Tavistock and Nottingham share the unique distinction of being the only towns in England still holding a Goose Fair. The origin of Tavistock's Goose Fair has been lost in time, but it is most certainly one of the oldest traditional fairs in Britain. There are conflicting theories concerning the history of Goose Fair, but little fact.

One theory holds that the word Goose is a corruption of the name Eustace or Eustachius, the Patron Saint of Tavistock parish church. An army officer during the early Roman Empire, he was celebrated for his military skill and bravery and was converted to Christianity after seeing the vision of a stag with a shining crucifix between its antlers in a forest near Preaneste in Italy. This vision is the subject of a magnificent painting by Pisanello in London's National Gallery. Because of his new faith Eustachius was driven from the army and after great suffering put to death in Rome. His Saint's day is 20 September.

Another theory associates Goose Fair with Michaelmas Day, for traditionally roast goose is Michaelmas fare and has been for centuries, as the Rev. Shaw discovered. He wrote of Tavistock in 1780 in his *A Tour to the West of England*: 'This being market day we met numbers of the people flocking hither with grain, a few sheep and an abundance of Michaelmas geese.'

There is evidence that for centuries Tavistock Goose Fair was held on Michaelmas Day and was an accepted part of this celebration, but to find what are now accepted as the real origins of the fair we must — as with almost everything pertaining to Tavistock — go back to the early days of the Benedictine Abbey of St Mary and St Rumon.

It is impossible to comprehend the spirit that has ensured the survival of Goose Fair without knowing something about the tremendous influence the Abbey had and for many people still has in the town.

THE BENEDICTINE ABBEY

As early as the tenth century on a site now occupied by part of the pannier market stood a chapel dedicated to St Matthew. In 974 Ordulf, brother-in-law of Edgar, the newly crowned 'undisputed King of all England', directed that a Benedictine Abbey be laid out alongside the River Tavy close to where the old road from Cornwall to Exeter crossed the water. In order not to offend the Cornish who even then displayed the individualism and pride that makes them a separate race to this day and who did not take kindly to the 'indiscipline' of the Benedictine Order, the Abbey was sited on the Devon side of the Tamar. But it was dedicated to a Cornish saint, St Rumon who, of course, like all good Cornish saints, was an Irishman. His remains were brought to Tavistock and enshrined in the Abbey church.

The building was completed by 981, but in 997 a raiding party of Danes sailed up the Tamar to attack Lydford and, being repulsed, sacked the Abbey on their way back, destroying it totally. Undaunted, Ordulf ordered it rebuilt and the resulting Abbey flourished until the Dissolution in 1539, spreading its civilising influence and culture throughout the whole of the South West.

In addition to self sacrifice and love of God, the monks somehow found the time to perform acts of great compassion and charity, giving warmth and shelter, food and clothing, to the poor and needy. Herbs grown in their own gardens were distilled in the Still House into medicine for the sick of the community. On the western outskirts of the town, they opened a leper hospital. The monks provided the only means of education for the young in the area, for the Abbey possessed one of the finest libraries in the land. By 1114, under Abbot Osbert, the power of the Abbey spread as far as the Isles of Scilly, where they built a small Priory on Tresco for two monks to administer these islands. The Abbey's possessions stretched from Dorset across Devon deep into Cornwall and included Manors, farms and estates.

Their farming techniques were revolutionary and highly successful and they introduced the process of 'thinning out' thick clay soil by mixing it with sand transported from South Devon by ship up the Tamar to Morwellham and then across country by packhorse. The first waterpowered corn mill in the South West was built by Tavistock Abbey, eliminating the burden of hand grinding. It is most likely these monks were the first to make Devonshire clotted cream in the manner still used today. To turn again to the Rev. Shaw, he commented: 'This essence of milk is gathered by scalding their whole quantity together in the state it comes from the cow, and letting it stand about a day, and then skimming off the top; by which means they have a greater quantity, but the milk is quite impoverished.' This was done to avoid wasting an excess of milk not required for butter, which they could not transport long distances.

The monks built 'fulling mills' for the woollen industry that developed in the thirteenth century, using running water to drive a water wheel attached to a revolving drum that alternately raised and dropped two wooden hammers on the cloth. This mechanical means of 'fulling' the cloth replaced the old methods of either squeezing it by hand, beating it with rods, or 'waulking' it in water-filled troughs tramping the wool flat by foot whilst still wet and shrinking it, thus increasing its natural tendency to 'felt' and mask the individual woollen threads.

The famous 'Tavistocks' made their appearance during the middle of the sixteenth century and were a version of the Devon Kersey of the Tiverton area, Exeter, Totnes and Ashburton. By 1618 Kerseys had developed into a principal export from the port of Exeter. It was also known as the Devon Dozen because of its length. This serge was made from coarse wool although little or nothing is known of the kind of sheep that provided it. With the gradual European preference for the finer quality wool of the Merino sheep and its introduction into this country, the coarser wool of the South West eventually became unobtainable and could only be purchased in Ireland. Tavistock's connection with the woollen industry continued — but on a smaller scale. In his book *The Rural Economy of the West of England*, William Marshall wrote in 1796: 'At Tavistock is a serge manufactory, but not I believe of any great extent and the spinning of worsted employs, of course, some of the female villagers in its neighbourhood.'

The last connection with this trade in Tavistock — a wool combing mill — finally closed in 1965. The industry that helped to build the town, and for many years the source of its prosperity, is now only remembered by a few words on a plaque near the mill site on Parkwood Road and by the 'Clothworkers' Aisle' in the parish church of

St Eustachius. This was donated by Constance, widow of wealthy merchant Maurice Bend, in 1445 and the stained glass window above the altar table in this aisle depicts St Martin, Patron Saint of all clothworkers.

Another outstanding achievement of this Benedictine Order occurred during the office of Abbot John Peryn, from 1523 to 1539. In his first year he introduced the earliest printing press seen in the South West and one of only seven throughout the Kingdom. A Tavistock-trained monk, Thomas Richard, working from the latin of Boethius took two years to print a translation of his *The Consolations of Philosophy*. He continued over the next ten years, it's believed, to print a Saxon Grammar and followed this with *The Statutes of the Stannaries*. It seems incredible and extremely sad that immediately after this last work was completed came the Dissolution and no other book of any kind was printed in Devonshire for a hundred and fifty years.

The Abbey's connection with Goose Fair originates most probably from the year 1105. The Abbot at that time was most likely Osbert, but this is difficult to verify. In return for a cash payment towards the cost of Henry I's war against the French, he obtained a Charter from the King confirming a weekly market to be held every Friday. Thereafter the first gaggles of geese were to be seen driven to market for sale along the lanes of Tavistock, particularly around Michaelmas when they were fat and in their prime. Tavistock market is still held on Friday today.

This market privilege granted to the Abbot was deeply resented by the more influential Barons in the County and they attempted to disrupt it causing the King to issue a second warrant commanding 'that the Abbot of Tavistock shall have his market in peace . . . and that no one is to do him wrong on that account.'

During Easter 1116 a third Charter was granted confirming this market and also granting a Fair in celebration of the feast of St Rumon for three days from 29 to 31 August.

The market and fair provided a useful source of income to the Abbot for he was entitled to extract a toll from both merchant and customer. Also during the fair monies due to the Abbey over the past year from tenants, farmers, craftsmen and tradesmen were paid, very often in kind, which always included a large number of geese. These, in common with other stock surplus to the Abbey's requirements, were then resold by the monks and the day on which this occurred has become accepted as Goose Fair day. The practice continued for many years during August, but some time after the Dissolution the date for Goose Fair was altered to Michaelmas Day. In 1823 Goose Fair day was finally changed to the second Wednesday in October and thus it has remained to the present day.

RIVER TAVY

To understand the size and character of the Abbey and better appreciate Tavistock and the people who over the years have fashioned and shaped it, why not take yourselves for a quiet walk along the banks of the Tavy away from the bustle of the Fair. You enter the relative calm of the riverside from Abbey Bridge, where even today boys are fishing from the parapet seemingly unaware of the hysteria and confusion that surrounds them. Their attention is centred around the floats bobbing in the peat-stained water under the arches, whose sudden disappearance announces the prospect of a fish on the hook.

Fishing from Abbey Bridge has been a practice among native born Tavistock youth for generations. Writing in his *Highways and Byways in Devon and Cornwall*, Arthur H. Norway in 1897 described the scene 'as the true centre of the Town of Tavistock, a wondrous place for reflection and romance. Here idleness is a virtue; and he is a bad man who hastens by with no more than a passing thought for the brown water foaming under the old bridge, the dark pools round which it whirls, the trailing ivy which hangs in the cool shadow of the arches, the weir over which the river boils a few yards further on, the salmon ladder by its side, and the leaping of fish in the still pool beyond, where the rush and turmoil of the fall is carried under water by its own weight and the foam and bubbles may be seen glistening below the unrippled surface.'

This glorious River Tavy starts its life at Tavy Head near Cranmere Pool under Cut Hill, twisting and turning its way across Dartmoor. It links with Amicombe Brook at Sandy Ford, making a 'U' turn into the splendour of the gorge at Tavy Cleave. Then flowing between Ger Tor and Standon Hill, it bequeaths its name to the sister and brother villages of Peter and Mary Tavy before bestowing the same privilege on Tavistock.

It clears the moor under Abbey Bridge, running on to join the Tamar at Bere Ferrers, where it flows with the Lynher through the

Hamoaze into Plymouth Sound. Such a river deserves a poet to sing its praises and proclaim its beauty to the world and the Tavy is lucky to have had William Browne, who lived from 1590 to 1645. A Tavistock-born contemporary of John Ford, he was educated at Tavistock Grammar School and Exeter College, Oxford. An admirer of the works of Edmund Spenser, he strove to emulate his pastoral style, succeeding in part with *Britannia's Pastorals*, his best known work. His passion for the countryside, particularly of his native Devon, was unequalled, and in this short passage he brilliantly captures the movement and imagery of running water.

Tavy creeps upon
The western vales of fertile Albion,
Here roughly dashes on an aged rock
That his intended passage doth up-lock;
There intricately 'mongst the woods doth wander,
Losing himself in many a wry meander;
Here amorously bent, clips some fair mead;
And then dispers'd in rills, doth measure tread
Upon her bosom 'mongst her flow'ry ranks.

He also tells of the activities associated with the Tavy water as it passes through village and town on its way to the sea.

Here stands a bridge and there a conduit head;
Here round a Maypole some the measure tread;
There boys the truant play and leave their book;
Here stands an angler with a baited hook;

Here stands the angler still with baited hook, his view along the river unchanged for centuries. You have the same view as you take the broad tree-lined path, running away west. The crenellated Abbey wall flanks the old herb garden on your right, and the still house where the monks distilled medicines in a two-storeyed tower marks the point where the Abbey building changed direction towards the west gate.

Continue on under a canopy of chestnuts, limes, ash and sycamore resplendent in their early autumn colours reflected in the waters of the Tavy. Through the topmost branches of four Lawsons Cypresses the lights of the Big Wheel constantly rotating remind you that Whitelegg's Fair sprawls over the entire area of the public carpark between the wharf and the river.

ALL THE FUN OF THE FAIR

There are people alive today who remember Goose Fair before Whiteleggs came to town. Then it was Hancock's Fair that provided the entertainment, arriving from Plymouth with rides and side-shows. They were drawn by teams of horses, four to a team, on steep hills doubling up to eight. They assisted the brakes on the way down by wedging long poles against the wheels.

Hancocks had the original Golden Gallopers, with a hand-wound organ, and a switchback on rails. The stalls gave away broken pieces of seaside rock as prizes with four pieces as a major award. The sideshows were lit by naphtha lamps of burnished brass and the most important task on arrival was finding a field for rest and provision of the horses. The site was a field near the old gasworks — an industrial estate today. Later it moved to the wharf with the fair-ground spreading itself along the bank of the river.

Hancock's Fair came to a violent end some time before the first world war whilst in Richmond Walk across Halfpenny Bridge in Plymouth. They were the victims of an attack by Suffragettes who burnt the Fair to the ground, thus ending a happy association with Tavistock and its people.

Many of Hancock's personnel joined Whiteleggs and continued their relationship with Goose Fair, replacing the horses with steam traction engines capable of pulling several trucks at once, each truck weighing between ten and twenty tons. Travelling at speeds of two to four miles an hour, it took a day to complete the journey from Ply-mouth to Tavistock. So heavy and difficult was the steering, it required two people to undertake it, often husband and wife working together. The weight created other problems, for the original iron wheels ripped up the roads, causing the Council to ban them until solid rubber tyres were fitted. These were not entirely successful and only the introduction of the internal combustion engine saved the Fair from extinction.

Not immediately, however, for the first motor wagons had an embarrassing habit of overheating, particularly on steep hills, causing the women to walk behind ready the moment the vehicles came to a halt to roll large boulders under the wheels to prevent them rolling backwards, for the brakes could never hold them.

What a difference today with thirty ton laden Scammel show trucks, complete with generators towing the components of side-shows, stalls, Big Wheel, Dodgems, ghost train, and all the other ingredients that constitute the 'fun of the fair', but alas I am sad to relate without that once so popular entertainment of all fairgrounds — the Boxing Booth. Mickey Kiely, who toured for many years with Whiteleggs, is now retired.

The life of showpeople is not for the workshy. The very word 'grafter', referring to hard work, originated in the fairground, and with justification. Theirs is not an easy life and, contrary to popular belief, few are likely to retire with an embarrassment of riches. The carnivals, fairs and regattas of the South West would be much less attractive without the travelling fair and its people, who for a brief time bring fun and an element of risk and uncertainty into the conformity of our standardised existence.

The show people cannot imagine a time when they might cease to travel the Westcountry from fair to fair. In the words of one of their number, Louvaine Lock, 'I certainly wouldn't like to think of that happening. We've been doing it all our lives. This is our life. Of course it gets more difficult every year finding sites to go to — that's the problem. Some people think we come free and don't have to pay anything for our fairground pitch, but that's not so. We do pay and it gets dearer each time. Sometimes our rent has increased fifty percent from the last year and we don't take that kind of money. I hope it will go on, as we've made so many friends. We know lots of people, and everywhere we go we have friends. Here in Tavistock we know almost everybody. I would hate to think of a time when we didn't come to Tavistock Goose Fair — something would have gone out of all our lives.'

Indeed it would, and I hope for all our sakes that day never arrives.

Continue your walk past the wall enclosing the fairgound to the Meadows, through a village of caravans — the only homes show people know and many are reluctant to give up on their retirement. Cross the Meadows to the canal built by John Taylor, an engineering genius, whose achievements in Tavistock have never been fully appreciated. He built the canal which was opened in 1817 linking the Tavy with the Tamar. It carried the mineral wealth of the area, the richest copper deposits in Europe which in 1856 amounted to 29,000 tons of ore handled on the quays at Morwellham.

30. Riding at the Fair

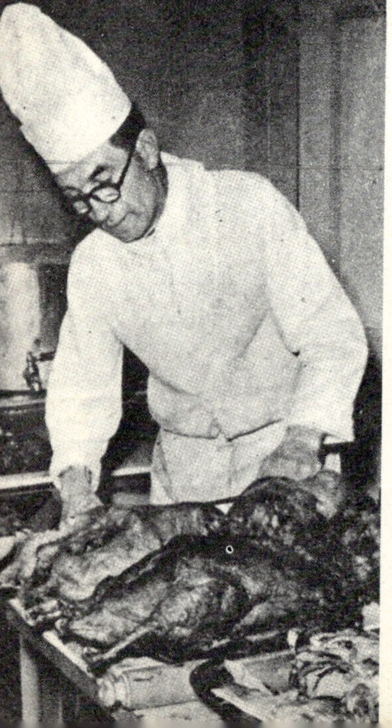

31-33 GOOSE DINNERS 1950s

▲ This is where they queued gladly.

◄ This is what they queued for.

▼ And this is how they enjoyed it.

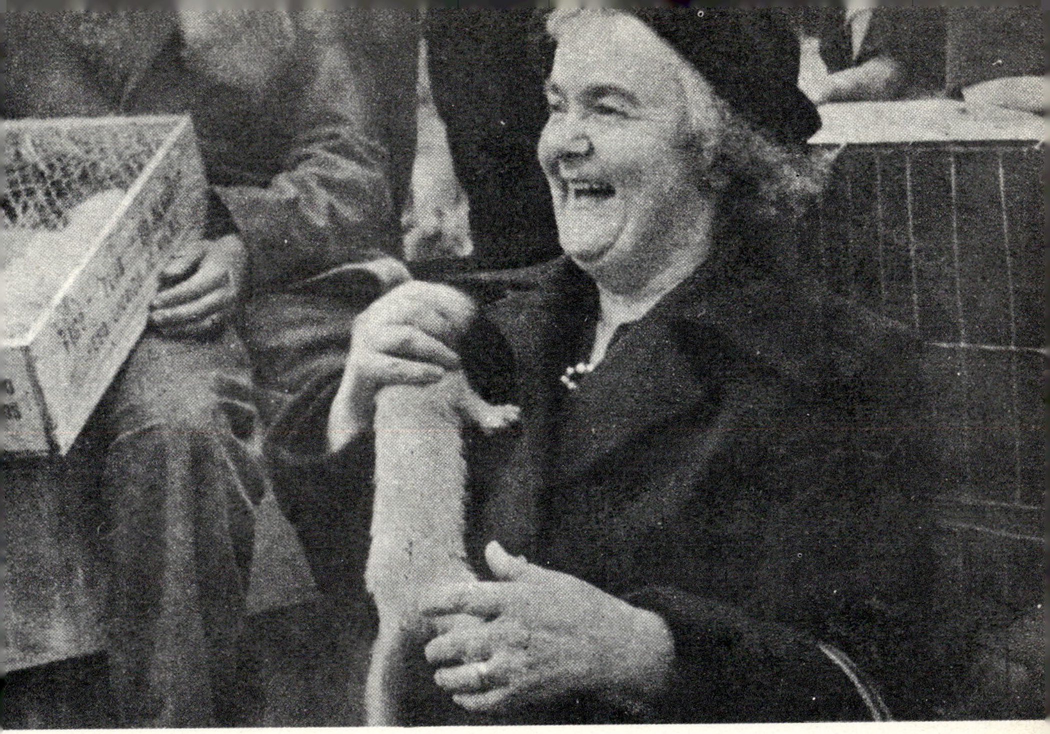

▲ 34. Ferrets too

35. The Old Shepherd: when asked his name said 'Everyone knows me.' They did - but no-one knew his name! ▼

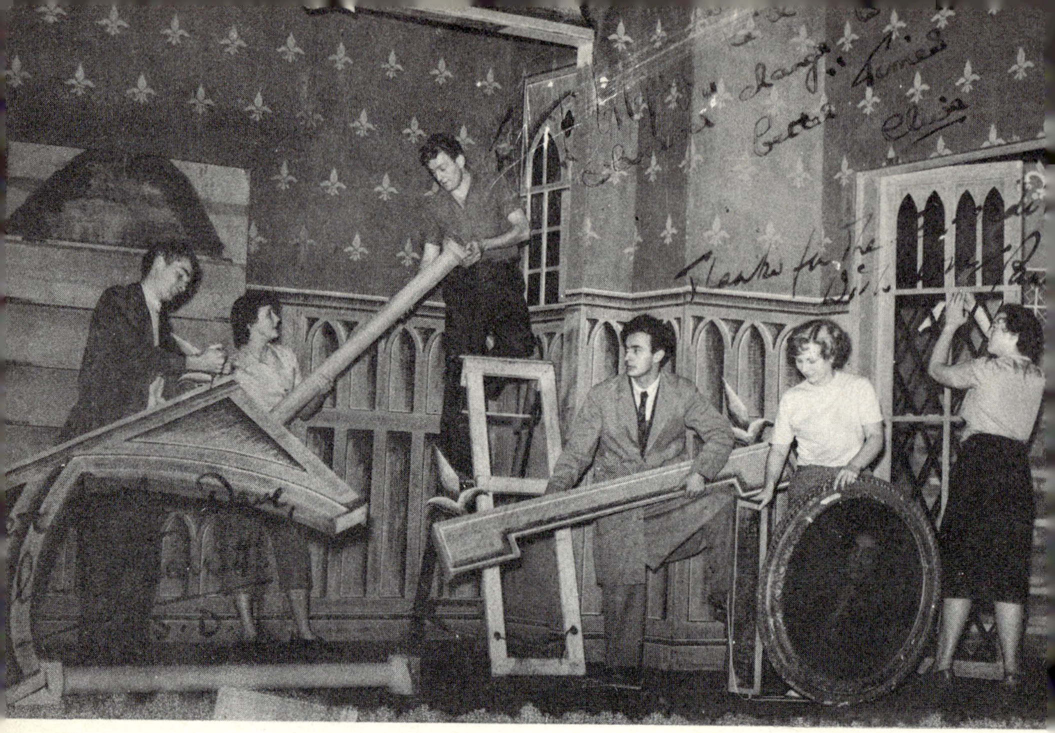

▲ 36. Clive Gunnell on the ladder: Nottingham Playhouse

37. The Fair 1950 ▼

38. 8 minutes past 11

39. Interior of Betsy Grimbal's Tower

40. From the top of Betsy's Tower

41. The Parish Church of St Eustachius

SIR FRANCIS DRAKE

Walk by the canal to the gate opening on to the Plymouth Road opposite the statue of Sir Francis Drake, where the plaque reads: 'Francis Drake, the Famous Navigator and Admiral, was born at Crowndale in the Tavistock Parish, about 1542 and died at Sea in 1596. This statue by Boehm was erected in 1883 through the generosity of Hastings, Ninth Duke of Bedford.'

The site of his birthplace Crowndale Farm lies a mile away past the Comprehensive School. All the visitor sees today of the original farm is the remains of one gable end with a small plaque recording Drake's birth and scattered around the ruins of the old smithy and well. The records of Tavistock Abbey show members of the Drake family living at Crowndale from 1481 when it was leased by Simon Drake, who was instructed by the Abbot, 'if he wishes to burn any portion of the land then he must apply sand or dung thereto in the same year, as is the custom of the countryside.'

Nothing authentic, however, is known of the circumstances of Drake's birth or his childhood to the age of five. It is believed that Drake's father Edmund worked for Lord Russell as a shepherd, marrying a Tavistock girl who bore him twelve children, the eldest being Francis. At his christening in the Parish Church of St Eustachius, it is said, Francis Russell, son of John, Lord Russell, stood as Godfather, but the Parish Church have no existing records of such a baptism.

Around the base of Boehm's statue are plaques depicting scenes from Drake's life including the grossly exaggerated game of bowls and, of course, his Knighthood. In this scene, as in the bronze in the Prince's Chamber in the House of Lords and many paintings of the same subject, the artist shows Queen Elizabeth laying the sword on Drake's shoulder. This honour she did not personally bestow, for being a woman of immense political acumen she cleverly contrived that the French Ambassador, who had accompanied her to Greenwich, perform the ceremony. Obviously an Ambassador could not refuse a Queen and his action in the eyes of the world stamped the French seal of approval on Drake's actions. Another plaque shows Drake buried at sea off Porto Bello. Here the artist shows his body wrapped in a hammock entering the water, but accounts of his death state that his body was put in a coffin.

His body being put into a Coffin of Lead, was let down into the sea, the trumpets in doleful manner Echoing out their Lamentations for so great a Loss and all the Cannons in the Fleet were discharged, according to the Custom of all Sea-Funeral Obsequies.

Thou that hast sailed the straits that lie beneath each Sun,
And those as well that may be traversed 'neath each pole;
Oh Drake, for thee I heaven's high shores felicitate,
Though in thy death indeed our own lot I must mourn.

THE ABBEY RUINS

Leaving Drake's statue behind, head back along the Plymouth Road towards the town centre, past the Drake Bowling Club and Tennis Courts. You quickly become engulfed once again by the crowds and confusion of Goose Fair which encroach almost to the Meadows. In the foreground stall owners and cheap jacks, haggle and bargain, coax and barter their wares to a gullible public at give-away prices! The crowds, mesmerised by this fascinating display of china and linen, toilet goods and jewellery, watches and toys, are totally unaware that hidden from view behind this show are the remains of the best in Tavistock's history.

In the front garden of the Vicarage are the remains of Betsy Grimbal's Tower, a name derived perhaps from a Nun called Betsy who was first loved and then murdered by a soldier, or it is more likely a corruption of Blessed Grimbald, a ninth century saint. Betsy Grimbal's is the southern of two towers framing the west gate of Tavistock Abbey which supported an upper room above the gateway. The northern tower was connected by passageway to the once very handsome Abbot's Lodgings. From here the Abbey wall continued across the Plymouth Road turning at right angles eastward and carrying on to adjoin the Abbey Church.

Turn right around and gaze past the stalls to the Parish Church. In the foreground, with the untrodden green of the churchyard as its mount stands all that remains of an Early English arch that once formed part of a colonnade running the length of the Abbey Church, making the northern line of the cloisters and ending at Court Gate in Bedford Square. This elegant gate still retains a great deal of its thirteenth century character and architecture with fifteenth century embellishments. Through here passed all visitors to the Abbey —

weary travellers, tradesmen and pilgrims seeking rest and shelter—to be met by the Guest Master, a monk whose duty it was to entertain guests with the best hospitality the Abbey could afford.

Try for a few seconds to picture this scene divorced from its present day Goose Fair reality and return to that age when the Abbey was at the peak of its power and influence in the area. Here where you are standing in the cloisters imagine the sun has etched reflections of the colonnade on the south wall of the Abbey church, a solitary monk sitting in its shade at work on a manuscript. Through columned openings at the east end you would see the architectural brilliance of the octagonal Chapter House. With its thirty-six arched stalls, it was used for all formal assemblies. Monks can be glimpsed in the dormitory and the sounds of preparations for a meal are coming from the Great Kitchen next to the Refectory. Outside the gate an enormous wheel drives the grinding stones of the Mill powered by the River Tavy, which also supplies water for the Abbey fish ponds, drainage and sanitation. Monks are engaged in the vegetable and herb gardens whilst others cart timber for building and fuel across the Abbey Bridge from the thickly wooded slopes of the south bank. The voices of monks at service in one of their compulsory eight daily prayers come from the Choir of the Abbey Church, a most beautiful building with a red and white clay tiled floor and white plaster walls bearing murals and decorations in red, yellow and black.

In the midst of these romantic reflections try to imagine the feelings of that good man, Abbot John Peryn, on Monday 3 March 1539 as he sat facing the Royal Commissioner appointed by Henry VIII to take surrender of the Monastery, its books, documents, and all its buildings, lands and possessions. Imagine his horror as he was then forced to watch the Church roof almost immediately stripped of its lead, the glass removed from the windows which were left open to the elements or stuffed up with straw, and the removal of all that was of value or use to the community of Tavistock. Within a hundred years of this act of Royal vandalism, the Abbey was fit only for demolition.

Three months after the surrender the whole parish of Tavistock was granted to John, Lord Russell, and thus began the second great influence in Tavistock's history. The Russells became the Dukes of Bedford with William, the fifth Earl, in 1694. They did not impose architectural awareness of their autocratic reign until the nineteenth century when Francis, 7th Duke of Bedford, immensely rich from the profits of mining activities covering acres of his land, began a rash of building projects throughout the town. He remodelled the town centre in Gothic style, the Guildhall in 1848, the Town Hall and pannier market between 1840 and 1860. He laid out the new Plymouth Road from Bedford Square to Fitzford Gateway and in the ten years between 1840 and 1850 built a hundred miners' cottages at a cost of £22 each from Fitzford to West Bridge. Finally, retaining the Gothic style, he remodelled what is now the Bedford Hotel, built originally by Jacob Saunders, merchant, as his private house in 1725 on the ruins of the Abbey Chapter House and Refectory. At the beginning of the nineteenth century it became an inn and the dining room still retains qualities of Saunder's original home.

Tavistock's once famous corn market, today a supermarket, was built during this period, as was the old workhouse, a splendid building designed by Sir Gilbert Scott. It is now converted into modern flats. Here the most celebrated of convicted murderers, Babbacombe Lee, lived out the remainder of his life as a pauper after his release from the death cell. He was pardoned after the trap under the gallows failed three times to spring open beneath his feet although working perfectly each time with sandbags. Having cheated the hangman, he is buried under the trees in Tavistock's old cemetery in Dolvin Road.

Having completed your walk, stand in Bedford Square, in my opinion one of the least spoiled and most beautiful town squares in England. Only a person of immense insensitivity can stand here in the warm quiet of an early summer morning and not feel deep within a response to the atmosphere of these surroundings and if that overworked word 'vibrations' has any true relevance in our lives, here surely is where the receptive soul will receive them.

THE PARISH CHURCH

You must choose how to spend the rest of your Goose Fair day, for the celebrating will continue long into the darkness and chill of this October night. Should you feel need for rest and retreat from the jostling crowd and pandemonium, cross the road from the Town Hall and enter the wooden gate taking the path through the churchyard into the Parish Church of St Eustachius, dedicated in 1318. It dominates the centre of Tavistock and is the burial place of Ordulf, founder of Tavistock Abbey. Six hundred years ago on a chilly January morning, the Abbot of Tavistock Abbey led a party of his household staff across from the Abbey Church to the Parish Church, bursting in on the vicar and, pulling him from his stall, slashed his vestments with their swords, and flung him out of his own Church. All this was to decide which of the two Churches was entitled to benefit from the collection.

No such violence will shatter your solitude today, however, even the din of Goose Fair is deadened by the thickness of the external walls built of green Hurdwick stone. In the Lady Chapel, dedicated to the Blessed Virgin Mary, is the Glanville memorial, the tomb of Sir John Glanville who died in 1600. He was born in Tavistock, and was the first attorney to reach the judicial bench. Dressed in his robes he reclines full length resting on one arm gazing fondly at his wife who kneels in front in an attitude of prayer, magnificently carved in alabaster. This is a unique example of early realism in sculpture and is a social study of a celebrated man and his family. The inscription which is in Latin reads: 'Sacred to the honoured memory of John Glanville, late one of the justices of the Common Pleas: who being deservedly made a Judge, administered justice with greatest labour, with justice maintained peace, in peace awaited death and in death found rest the 27 day of July in the year of our Lord 1600.'

When you leave the Church to stand once again in Bedford Square watching the Golden Gallopers continuously running their endless race to nowhere, your senses lulled by the nostalgic chords of the Gavioli organ, surrounded by a dense crowd of expectant people, pushing and shoving, laughing and shouting, allow yourselves one minute to recall that somewhere buried under all this excitement beneath the tarmac road surface laid over the Abbey cloisters and Chapter House, sleep dedicated monks who during five hundred years of Tavistock's history devoted their lives to God's service and left behind, for all who are aware and care, their sole possessions in life, love and spiritual presence. Some of that presence still exists in Tavistock today, for whatever you do on Goosie Fair day, wherever you go, there will be a welcome and the opportunity to fulfill all your eager expectations. If this is your first visit you will make many friends, if you have been before you will consolidate old friendships and make new, for it will be a day to remember, a day you will look forward to next year. You will not forget Tavistock and you will return.

For the benefit of those pessimists who are continuously telling us, 'Goosie Fair is not as good as it was in the old days — it's had its day', let me close not with my own words but those of one of the best known figures in the town of Tavistock, Mr Eric Kingdon. Historian, member of the Devonshire Association and an accepted authority on the town, he was for some time Editor of the *Tavistock Gazette* which for 117 years was the epitome of all a country town newspaper should be. Eric Kingdon has been honoured for his services to the town for the new Community Centre, now being renovated in the old Gazette works at Plym Street, is named after him.

Writing in an editorial some time ago, he used words that absolutely convey my own feelings for Tavistock, its history, traditions and people, a love I have tried to illustrate in this book.

'We have mused over the dear dead days beyond recall, re-living some of our joys and finding renewed poignancy in some of our sorrows.

'Through reading all this we realise we have inherited a goodly heritage.

'We found a widely varying collection of happenings; oft-times comedy and tragedy follow close upon each other's heels, the laughter and tears, in the strange thing we call life.'

When I asked Eric Kingdon whether he thought Goose Fair was as good now as in the past and could continue to survive, he made this reply. 'Many people you know say, "Oh, Goosie Fair is not as good as it used to be. It will not survive much longer."

'They remind me of the man who wrote a letter to the editor of *Punch* saying, "Sir, your magazine isn't half so funny as it used to be."

'The editor sent him back a postcard with written on it: "It never was!"

'Oh! Goosie Fair will survive and flourish, never fear.'

ALSO BY CLIVE GUNNELL

MY DARTMOOR

by Clive Gunnell of Westward TV — television's most famous walker. Price 95p. Map and 12 pages of photographs and drawings of Dartmoor wildlife by Robin Armstrong. Introduction by Jeremy Thorpe, M.P.

". . . a winner all the way . . ." Express & Echo

"The work is that of a merry man, and an observant, though kindly one." Western Morning News

"An excellent book." Kenneth MacLeod on Westward TV

". . . fascinating reading . . ." Plymouth Times

Clive Gunnell and the Moor . . . the love affair that will never end . . ." Jim Dalrymple, The Independent

TITLES BY ELIZABETH GUNNELL

THE BARBICAN

32 photographs Price 65p

"Anyone with a love for old Plymouth and the waterfront should not miss this lovely little book. It is outstanding value and highly recommended." Tavistock Gazette

". . . packed full of treasures from the Barbican's characters . . . to its latter-day activities, as well as a host of information . . ." Westcountryman

TOTNES

32 illustrations Price 65p

Elizabeth Gunnell follows the success of her Barbican story with an immensely readable guide about Totnes, one of the oldest boroughs in Britain.

"We meet historic people cheek-by-jowl with moderns . . . they all step out of the pages equally alive." Devon Life

OTHER TITLES INCLUDE

BOTH SIDES OF TAMAR

Devon & Cornwall portrayed in words and pictures. 24 illustrations. Price 95p. Chapters by John Betjeman, Charles Causley, J.C. Trewin, Clive Gunnell, Tom Salmon, E.W. Martin, Bill Best Harris, James Turner, Jane Toplis and Arthur Caddick.

". . . a memorable book on Devon and Cornwall." Western Morning News

". . . a dazzling array of talent." Arthur Venning, Editor, Cornish & Devon Post

ALONG THE LEMON

By Judy Chard. 35 photographs and map. Price 65p.
The lifestory of a Dartmoor river by the well-known Devon novelist and short story writer who lives alongside it. Judy Chard puts one of Devon's lesser-known rivers on the map, tracing its journey from below Haytor to where it meets the Teign at Newton Abbot.

TIGHTLINES SOUTH WEST

A fishing guide to the south west by the popular Westcountry and Westward TV angler. Drawings and photographs — a mine of information for the angler, both local and visitors. 95p.
"A book with Tightlines South West as its title can only have been written by one person. And Ted Tuckerman doesn't disappoint us. He shares his vast knowledge of angling and where to fish our local shores and wrecks."

Jack White, Sunday Independent

MURDER IN THE WESTCOUNTRY

introduced by Colin Wilson. 16 photographs. Price 95p.
Ten famous murder cases.
"This murderous excursion from Bude to Bristol and beyond is recommended as compelling reading."

Colin Haxton, Southern Evening Echo

ABOUT EXMOOR AND NORTH DEVON

by Ronald Duncan. 15 photographs and map. Price 65p.
"You will find this book well-informed, well-written, well-illustrated and provocative."

The John Blunt Column

". . . suggested routes across some of the loveliest stretches of the Westcountry."

Western Daily Press

MY CORNWALL

A personal vision of Cornwall by eleven writers living and working in the county: Daphne du Maurier, Ronald Duncan, James Turner, Angela du Maurier, Jack Clemo, Denys Val Baker, Colin Wilson, C.C. Vyvyan, Arthur Caddick, Michael Williams and Derek Tangye with reproductions of paintings by Margo Maeckelberghe and photographs by Bryan Russell. Price 95p.
"An ambitious collection of chapters."

The Times, London

SUPERNATURAL IN CORNWALL

by Michael Williams. 24 photographs. Price £1.50.
". . . a book of fact, not fiction . . . covers not only apparitions, and things that go bump in the night, but also witchcraft, clairvoyancy, spiritual healing, even wart charming . . ." Jenny Myerscough on BBC